Swantje We

"Shooting an Elephant" of George Orwell - Short Story or E   ence of Colonialism?

GRIN - Verlag für akademische Texte

Der GRIN Verlag mit Sitz in München hat sich seit der Gründung im Jahr 1998 auf die Veröffentlichung akademischer Texte spezialisiert.

Die Verlagswebseite www.grin.com ist für Studenten, Hochschullehrer und andere Akademiker die ideale Plattform, ihre Fachtexte, Studienarbeiten, Abschlussarbeiten oder Dissertationen einem breiten Publikum zu präsentieren.

Dokument Nr. V170862 aus dem GRIN Verlagsprogramm

Swantje We

"Shooting an Elephant" of George Orwell - Short Story or Essay on the Essence of Colonialism?

GRIN Verlag

Bibliografische Information der Deutschen Nationalbibliothek: Die Deutsche Bibliothek
verzeichnet diese Publikation in der Deutschen Nationalbibliografie; detaillierte bibliografische Daten sind im Internet über http://dnb.d-nb.de/ abrufbar.

1. Auflage 2010
Copyright © 2010 GRIN Verlag
http://www.grin.com/
Druck und Bindung: Books on Demand GmbH, Norderstedt Germany
ISBN 978-3-640-90083-1

Universität Vechta
University of Vechta

Institut für Geistes- und Kulturwissenschaften
Sommersemester 2010
Seminar: Fields of Literary Studies
Option I: George Orwell

"Shooting an Elephant": Short Story or Essay on the Essence of Colonialism?

Table of Contents

1. Introduction 3
2. Definitions 3
   2.1. Definition 'Essay' 3
   2.2. Definition "Short Story" 4
3. Plot Summary 4
4. Analysis 5
   4.1. Arguments for the Essay 5
      4.1.1. Parallels to Orwell's Biography 5
      4.1.2. Parallels between Orwell and the Narrator 6
   4.2. The narrator's conflict 7
   4.3. The Symbol of the Elephant 8
   4.4. Roll-Call 9
5. Arguments for the Short Story 9
   5.1. Construction 9
      5.1.1. Title, Beginning and Ending 11
6. Conclusion 12
Sources 14

1. Introduction

This paper deals with Orwell's text 'Shooting an Elephant'. I use the term *text* deliberately since my topic says "George Orwell: 'Shooting an Elephant' - Short Story or Essay on the Essence of Colonialism". The question of genre has been debated for decades and there have been several quarrels about allocating it to a certain genre. Most experts, however, call the text an *essay* but there are also those who insist on the text belonging to the group of the *short stories*.

In my paper I will work out features of both genres and at the end of my study I will sum up the findings and draw a conclusion.

First, I will give a short definition of the terms 'Short Story' and 'Essay'. This is to show the characteristics of the two genres that I will pick up again in the course of this paper. After a brief summary I will start the analysis of the text working out topics like parallels to Orwell's life, the meaning of the elephant or the construction of the text. In the final part I will sum up my results and draw a conclusion.

2. Definitions

2.1. Definition 'Essay'

To start with, I will define the term 'Essay' to show the characteristic features of that genre. An *essay* is non-fictional prose. It is always influenced by the author's opinion and therefore subjective. The author reflects about the past, comments on the action or judges several topics. Thus, there are mostly parallels to the author's own life.

The essayist aims to address the reader in a language anyone is able to understand easily. Moreover, there is no predefined pattern how to structure the text. The author is free to choose his individual style and topic, whereas the reader should be able to read the whole text in one stroke.

In the Anglo-Saxon area the term *essay* is used to describe all non-fictional literature1. Therefore, this paper will discuss the degree of personal reflection in this text[1].

An important hint concerning 'Shooting an Elephant' is the fact that the genre of the *essay* was connected with fictional genres in the course of the 20th century.

---

[1] For both definitions I refer to the German definition of Lamping/Poppe. I translated the definition and put it in my own words as good as possible.

2.2. Definition "Short Story"

In contrast to the *essay*, the *short story* is fictional prose. It is characterised by its shortness and the unity of time, setting and plot. The course of the action is limited to some kind of extract, for example a special event, a scene or even just a moment. The events do not need to follow a logical and chronological order but can occur out of context. Mostly, there is an abrupt beginning with the story starting *in medias res* and an open ending. The ending is often also an abrupt one similar to the ending of an anecdote with the storyline coming to a solution in the form of a punch line. Further, ending, title and beginning often contain central information regarding the analysis of the text. Therefore, the ending, title and beginning of 'Shooting an Elephant' will be discussed in detail in the course of this paper.

The characters presented in a *short story* are limited to only few in most cases and usually symbolise stock characters.

Regarding the perspective of narration, there is only one usually; changes of the perspective are uncommon.

Furthermore, the words employed are the ones needed, redundant words are left out.

3. Plot Summary

The story of 'Shooting an Elephant' takes place in Moulmein, Burma, during the time of British Imperial Leadership in India. The narrator is a British police officer who notices a strong anti-European feeling among the natives. Although a representative of British power, the narrator sympathises with the oppressed natives and their country but is forced to act according to imperial aims. This conflict is revealed by the central event of the story.

When the narrator receives a call, he is commissioned to bring an eloped elephant under control. In order to defend himself in case of an attack, he takes a rifle, which makes the natives think that the elephant is going to be shot. Once the narrator arrives, he finds a peaceful animal which offers no danger. Therefore, he decides not to shoot, but there is the mass of natives behind him that demands the police officer shooting the elephant. After an inner struggle, the narrator finally gives in to the power of the natives' demanding and shoots. It takes several shots for the animal to dye painfully. The officer cannot stand this scenery and leaves while the natives have already started tearing out

pieces of meat. He concludes stating that shooting the elephant was necessary as a means of demonstrating power and ensure British dominion.

4. Analysis
4.1. Arguments for the Essay
4.1.1. Parallels to Orwell's Biography

There are striking parallels between the story and Orwell's own life that support the argument for 'Shooting an Elephant' being an *essay*. The most striking and obvious parallel is the fact that Orwell himself served as a police officer in Burma from 1922 to 1927. He was educated at Eton and then volunteered to serve in India. His father had also worked as a police officer in *Moulmein* which can be seen as another striking parallel between the writer's family background and the setting of the story. Orwell definitely had a personal relation to *Moulmein*. His grandmother and his aunt Nora lived there and Orwell had come to visit them several times before his service for the Imperial Police started in 1922. Later, when Orwell served in Burma, he played football in the *Moulmein Police Team*. Regarding this fact, there is a reference in the text when he writes about "a nimble Burman tripping him on the football field" (Orwell 1). In this case, there is not only a personal relation to the place but also to personal interests and activities. He may even refer to his own experience as a British football player during his time in Burma.

While *Moulmein* is an obvious hint to a place Orwell knew, there is another hint to a place that had a remarkable impact on Orwell's thinking. In the text he writes about the terrible circumstances Burmese prisoners have to bear. In September 1925, he went to *Insein*, the city with the second-largest jail in Burma. This visit obviously touched Orwell's mind. He mentions

> "the wretched prisoners huddling in the stinking cages of the lock-ups [...] the men who had been flogged with bamboos – all these oppressed me with an intolerable sense of guilt" (Orwell 1)

in the text. This quote reveals the narrator as an Englishman who sympathises with the native population and who despises their brutal oppression.

His biographer writes about Orwell "Whatever he may subsequently have thought about the colonial administrators he was, with a few dramatic exceptions, charmed by the native population" (Taylor 67). His anti-imperialistic view becomes obvious once more when he makes the narrator state that "imperialism was an evil thing" (Orwell 1). This

statement brought by a servant of the Empire evokes the question of integrity but Orwell himself, though anti-imperialistic in his thinking, never revealed this attitude towards political order to his colleagues. None of his companions would ever have thought him opponent to imperialistic convictions. In 1929, two years after he had returned home, Orwell wrote in a French newspaper, "if we are correct, it is true that the British are robbing and pilfering Burma quite shamefully" (Taylor 69). Thus, the statement of the narrator in 'Shooting an Elephant' can be regarded as a statement of Orwell himself.

Moreover, the surroundings described are very similar to those Orwell found there when he served in Burma, few Englishmen trying to ensure power about the mass. Crime statistics of that time show that there was a lack of authority on the British side since the ruled began to stand up and rebel against their oppressors. There are some examples in the text that illustrate these circumstances. When he mentions the natives bating the British or putting juice over an Englishwoman's dress or when he writes about the prisoners in jail, he emphasises the differences between the ruling and the ruled.

Even for the central event of the story there is a parallel to Orwell's biography. George Stuart, a contemporary, claimed that he had been in the office when Orwell came to borrow an elephant rifle. Later, Orwell was transferred to Katha as a punishment for shooting an elephant (Quinn 42). There are, however, no official records for Stuart's claim.

4.1.2. Parallels between Orwell and the Narrator

Reading the text in front of Orwell's biographical background, the parallels between the narrator and the author are obvious. There is the profession of the Imperial Policeman that both of them share, the position as a representative of the British Empire in the East. Both do their job but do not agree with the idea of colonialism in its whole. Therefore, the narrator once points out, "As for the job I was doing, I hated it more bitterly than I can perhaps make clear" (Orwell 1). This shows his discontent with the situation and it makes clear that he is doing his job but does not act due to his own convictions but to those of his superior. Orwell also disliked the idea of colonialism strongly. After returning from Burma he voices his criticism against imperialism in several newspaper articles. Moreover, the reasons for his return to England are unclear. He did not resign from his service but left with a medical certificate. Illness, however, was never mentioned in the letters he wrote to his family in England. In 1940 he explained the

reasons for returning in a newspaper article stating that he left Burma "partly because the climate had ruined my health, partly because I could not go any longer serving an imperialism which I had come to regard as very largely a racket" (Taylor 76). This statement leads to the assumption that the medical certificate only acted as his ticket home and that Orwell had not been seriously ill but simply wanted to escape conditions he could no longer bear.

As for these conditions, the inequality between the natives and the British was something that was against Orwell's personal convictions although officially standing on the side of the rulers. When the narrator mentions the dramatic situation the prisoners are in it seems like the author himself was talking through the narrator. As said before, Orwell visited *Insein*, the city with the second-largest jail in Burma during his time of service for the Imperial Police and was deeply shocked by what he saw there. One can suspect that the impressions he got took some time to establish and that they found their expression in his work (Taylor 78). This is another argument for the *essay* since Orwell works up experiences.

In 1927 Orwell left Burma most probably due to his anti-imperialistic conviction. He was not content with his job and the circumstances he found in the East with the ruling British oppressing the natives. When the narrator points out that "imperialism was an evil thing and the sooner I chucked up my job and got out of it the better" (Orwell 1) or when he talks about "the hollowness, the futility of the white man's dominion in the East" (3) Orwell definitely draws a connection to his own thinking and acting. He was also discontent with his situation as a man who had to enforce obedience of the natives but did not even have their respect. At the time when Orwell served in Burma the situation was very critical. The Indians began to rebel against their oppressors and the representatives of British power were far too few to maintain control. That is why the Imperial Policemen were very busy ensuring superiority while the natives strived for freedom. The British had to demonstrate their power to make the natives devote to their word.

4.2. The narrator's conflict

When the narrator stands in front of the crowd of natives he is torn between his own convictions that there is no need to shoot and the demand of the crowd to kill the elephant. They have followed him the way up and now stand behind him excited about

the event[2]. The natives are keen to watch the British man demonstrate his superiority while the narrator still insists on not shooting the animal gratuitously. He asserts repeatedly that he will not shoot him for he knows that a working elephant is very valuable and that he "would only be worth the value of his tusks" (3) if he shot him.

When the narrator states, "I could feel their two thousand wills pressing me forward, irresistibly" (3) he notices the tension increasing and the strong demand for action. The conflict heats up and he realizes that he "should have to shoot the elephant" (3). The crowd's pressure contradicts with his decision and he realizes that the natives got control over him and that he is not "the leading actor of the piece" (3) any more but "an absurd puppet pushed to and fro by the will of those yellow faces behind" (3). He knows that shooting the elephant is the only chance to save face as an Imperial Policeman. If he does not kill the elephant, the image of the white man in the East will be destroyed. For it is his duty to impress the crowd as a means of ensuring dominion. That means that there is no chance to escape dignifiedly else shooting. Otherwise the natives would make fun of him and that would destroy every white man's reputation. The narrator has come to a point where he is responsible for the reputation of his compatriots. Shooting the elephant means demonstrating strength and power while a retreat would call into question the superiority of the British. Therefore, there is no other opportunity for the narrator but firing.

4.3. The Symbol of the Elephant

When the narrator has shot the elephant he points out, "He was dying, very slowly and in great agony, but in some world remote from me where not even a bullet could damage him further" (5). That means that the elephant has been shot by the narrator but still has not given in to his command. It is clear that the elephant will die but the narrator is not able to finish him. Orwell presents a very detailed description of the elephant's painful dying to highlight the cruelty of the narrator's action.

The elephant can be regarded as a symbol. On the one hand he is a very valuable working animal which offers the livelihood for his owner; on the other hand he is used as a means to demonstrate superiority. Therefore, the elephant dies innocently. When the narrator arrives he offers no danger any more and there is no need to kill him. The narrator, however, is put under pressure by the crowd of natives. He finally kills the

---

[2] "They had not shown much interest in the elephant when he was merely ravaging their homes but it was different now that he was going to be shot" (Orwell 3).

elephant in order to escape the situation and obeys to the will of the mass. Therefore, one can say that although the British are the oppressors usually, the narrator is oppressed by the crowd's demanding. The elephant is an innocent actor of the piece but he is the one to pay his live for the struggle between the ruling and the ruled. He becomes the victim of colonial struggles and is abused to negotiate the roles.

4.4. Roll-Call

Orwell aims to address the reader with a message. The reader knows that the only reason for shooting the elephant was the narrator's fear to lose face. He is urged to act according to the will of the natives who demand the shooting of the elephant. In this situation he is not free to act as he would like to but gives in to the will of the crowd.

The message Orwell wants to tell is that colonialism makes both, the British as well as the natives, unfree. Moreover, it causes innocent victims that lose their life for imperialistic aims and struggles. The narrator is enabled in his action since the crowd controls him mentally while the British oppress the Burmese physically[3]. The result, however, is the same. Both cannot act as they would like to and are caught in limitations and the pursuit of power. The British want to expand their powers, but in reality they reduce them by oppressing the natives.

The fact that Orwell embeds a role-call into his text strengthens the argument for an essay since this is a typical feature of this genre.

Therefore, from the content point of view, things are clearly speaking for the *essay*. That is why the construction of 'Shooting an Elephant' has to be considered.

5. Arguments for the Short Story

5.1. Construction

The construction of a text often reveals a lot about its genre. At the beginning of this paper the most important features of both genres have been mentioned.

The first point to work out is the unity of time, setting and plot. As for 'Shooting an Elephant' that this feature is fulfilled. *Moulmein* is the place where the story is set. Although the narrator has to move from his office to the field where the elephant is, the unity of place is not offended. The central event of the text, the struggle of shooting the elephant, fulfils the characteristic of one setting. From the point when the narrator

---

[3] 'Physically' in this case means by military dominance.

receives the call, the reader is witness of his actions. He accompanies the narrator on his way to the field with the ordering of an elephant rifle and the interviewing of the natives up to the arrival at the field where the central action begins.

As for the time, there are no flashbacks into the past or jumps into the future. The story follows a chronological order. There is one setting to one time with one plot.

These are arguments for a *short story*; however, an *essay* does not require a certain structure but is optional in the way it is built up. Therefore, claiming that these features alone would suffice as indicators for a *short story* is too vague. More features need to be examined.

The focus of the story is on the struggle of shooting the elephant. Therefore, the author focuses on one event only and presents an excerpt from the narrator's life in Burma. There is no special introduction to the setting and to surroundings; the reader does not even know the name of the person who is telling the story. The narrator informs the reader about his profession as a police officer in Burma but neither tells how long he has been doing his job nor does he reveal any information about his social background. Questions like those if the event presents a usual day are not answered. Moreover, the reader does not know anything about the rest of the day, the rest of the week or about the reaction of the people in the following days. He only gets insight into a few moments of a police officer's work in India and becomes witness of the narrator's conflict regarding the shooting of an elephant. This further manifests the argument for a *short story* construction but it still needs more features for reliance.

The narrator, however, is not the only character of the story. The mass of natives that pushes him to shooting the animal is only characterised by its action during the course of the event. In this case, the big face of the mass stands for three thousand Burmese. The crowd consists of many actors but there is no need to pick out single ones since they function as one power. There is no individual characterisation of each person but the different actors symbolise stock characters. This and the fact that the action is limited to a single event here also support the argument for a *short story*.

The perspective of narration is another aspect one has to take into consideration. In 'Shooting an Elephant' the perspective from which the story is told is clear. The narrator tells the reader about the events. From the first sentence on, we experience the world through the eyes of the Imperial Policeman. He is the only one telling the story from his point of view without any changes in the perspective.

The facts mentioned so far, however, do not unequivocally indicate that 'Shooting an Elephant' exhibits features which only fit for the genre *short story*. Up to now, the features worked out concerning the *essay* are more reliable. Therefore, the focus will be put on the beginning and ending of the text now.

5.1.1. Title, Beginning and Ending

Title, beginning and ending often contain information that is important for the story. To start with the title, 'Shooting an Elephant' does not only name the central event of the story but it also implies the role of the elephant. The shooting of the elephant causes trouble since the narrator's convictions compete with the crowd's demand. A long process of struggling and pressure bursts out into the final solution of killing the elephant. He is only shot for the narrator does not know another way to escape the pressure of the crowd behind him. He is forced to act and killing the animal is his only chance to safe face. Therefore, the elephant is rather used as a means or instrument to maintain superiority. It does not matter what the elephant is like or which animal it is. It has a function and this function can be fulfilled by any elephant. When Orwell titles his story 'Shooting *an* Elephant' the indefinite article implies this role of any animal which acts as a victim of competing interests.

As for the beginning of the story, the first sentence is kind of strange[4]. The narrator states that he "was hated by large numbers of people" (1) also adding that this caused him some kind of celebrity. This statement tells a lot about the story following. The narrator is a British Policeman and therefore, due to his profession, disliked by the majority of natives. This usual unpopularity, however, does not make him distinct to other British Policemen in Burma. The decisive hint is given by his supplement "the only time in my life that I have been important enough for this to happen to me" (1). This addition points to the development of the story. Namely, that something will happen that shapes the role of the narrator and provides him attention. In connection to the title of the text, the reader can imagine what event the narrator refers to. The first sentence, however, goes beyond the shooting and the inner struggle of the narrator. It reveals that no matter what the British Policeman does, he is always hated by the native population. When he has shot the elephant, the three thousand Burmans marching

---

[4] "In Moulmein, in lower Burma, I was hated by large numbers of people-the only time in my life that I have been important enough for this to happen to me." (Orwell 1)

behind him are pleased. Nevertheless, the owner and even some of the British condemn his action and he is not only hated by the natives but also by his compatriots now.

Regarding the ending of the story, there is a connection to the first sentence since it picks up indications that are made in the first sentence. The narrator concludes that he was relieved that the elephant had killed a native since this provided a reason for shooting him. Although this is a suitable justification for his action, some of his compatriots do strongly disagree with the narrator. In the last sentence, he points out that he had only killed the animal "to avoid looking a fool" (5). The narrator is disappointed of the reaction of the British since he pretends to have done it as a means to ensure British dominion and rescue the reputation of the British in the East.

It is unclear whether he tells them about his reasons later or not. The story ends and questions for further actions of the narrator remain unanswered. Therefore, the story does not really have an open ending but is also not closed in the whole since the narrator draws a conclusion that evokes new questions of the consequences.

Regarding the connection of title, beginning and ending one can conclude that this is a hint for a *short story* for it is consciously constructed. Orwell would not have needed to create a connection between these three elements for an *essay* where he simply wants to lecture the reader. His aim was to construct something artistic that unequivocally contains personal reflections about his time in Burma. He made use of artistic elements for aesthetic and rhetoric reasons since his aim was to offer inside knowledge into the wrongs of the empire (Meyers 24).

6. Conclusion

The question whether 'Shooting an Elephant' is a *short story* or an *essay* needs to be answered in diplomatic way. In the text we find a lot of hints for the essay if we take a look at the parallels between the events in the text and Orwell's biography or the parallels between Orwell and the narrator. There is no doubt that Orwell refers to his own experiences in Burma. In many cases it seems as if Orwell himself is telling his own story through the narrator.

Taking a look at the construction and body of the text, however, there are obvious hints for the *short story*. Above all, the way Orwell created a connection between title, beginning and ending points to elements of a short story.

As for the fact that Orwell makes the elephant the victim of contradictory interests, it is questionable whether he really experienced the event during his time in Burma. The

way he describes the painful process of the elephant's dying evokes doubts whether his description can be regarded as real.

At the beginning of this paper I said that there was a connection between the two genres in the 20th century. In this case this would be an adequate way to define the genre here. In 'Shooting an Elephant' one finds both, features of a *short story* in the construction of the text as well as those of an *essay* in the content. Summarising I can say that the text has the construction of a *short story* but is an *essay* from the content side. It is an example for a text where both genres have been mixed up. Therefore, Valerie Meyer calls 'Shooting an Elephant' a "narrative essay" (24).

Sources

Primary Literature

Orwell, George, *Shooting an Elephant* (downloaded)

Secondary Literature

Bounds, Philip, *Orwell and Marxism: The political and cultural thinking of George Orwell.* London (u.a.): I.B. Tauris, 2009

Knellwolf King, Christa, *Stories of empire: narrative strategies for the legitimation of an imperial world order.* Conference "Studies of Empire"; (Wien): 2007.09. Trier: WVT, Wiss. Verl. Trier, 2009

Lamping, Dieter and Poppe, Sandra, *Handbuch der literarischen Gattungen.* Stuttgart: Kröner, 2009

Meyers, Valerie, *George Orwell.* New York: St. Martin's Press, 1991

Parry, Benita, *Delusions and discoveries: India and the British imagination, 1880-1930.* London (u.a.): Verso, 1998

Quinn, Edward, *Critical Companion to George Orwell: a literary reference to his life and work.* New York, NY: Facts on File, 2009

Rodden, John (ed.), *The Cambridge Companion to George Orwell.* Cambridge (u.a.): Cambridge Univ. Press, 2009

Rodden, John, with a new introduction and glossary by the author, *The politics of literary reputation.* 3rd Print. New Brunswick, NY (u.a.): Transaction Publishers, 2006

Singh, Rashna Batliwala, *The imperishable Empire: a study of British fiction on India.* Washington, D.C.: Three Continents Press, 1988

Taylor, David John, *The Life.* London: Vintage Books, 2004

Viswanathan, Gauri, *Masks of Conquest: a literary study and British rule in India.* London: Faber and Faber, 1989

Lightning Source UK Ltd.
Milton Keynes UK
UKIC01n2247090913
216877UK00001B